BETTER DATA MODELING:
AN INTRODUCTION TO AGILE DATA
ENGINEERING USING DATA VAULT 2.0

Kent Graziano

Data Warrior LLC

http://kentgraziano.com

Better Data Modeling:

An Introduction to Agile Data Engineering

Using Data Vault 2.0

Copyright © 2015-2021, Kent Graziano

Table of Contents

Chapter 1: Agile Data Engineering - Not an Option Anymore

The world is changing.

No – *the world as we knew it in IT **has** changed.*

Big Data & Agile are hot topics.

But companies still need to **collect**, **report**, and **analyze** their data. Usually this requires some form of data warehousing or business intelligence system. So how do we do that in the modern IT landscape in a way that allows us to be **agile** and either deal directly or indirectly with unstructured and semi structured data?

First off, we need to change our evil ways – we can no longer afford to take years to deliver data to the business. We cannot spend months doing detailed analysis to develop use cases and detailed specification documents. Then spend months building enterprise scale data models only to deploy them and find out the source systems changed and the models have no place to hold the now-relevant data critical to business success.

We have to be more agile than that.

We need a way to do **Agile Data Engineering** if we ever expect to achieve the goal of **Agile Data Warehousing**.

The **Data Vault System of Business Intelligence** provides (among other things) a method and approach to modeling your enterprise data warehouse (EDW) that is agile, flexible, and scalable.

Why Data Vault?

Current approaches to modeling a data warehouse include developing **3rd Normal Form** (3NF) type models or dimensional **star schema** models. Now while there are indeed architects and modelers out there who have been wildly successful using these approaches, there are many more that have failed, and failed big.

Why? Mostly lack of experience, but more so that these approaches have some basic issues that while resolvable, do require a certain level of **engineering expertise** that is not readily available in the industry today (and is declining daily).

What are these issues?

In the **usual 3NF** approach, in order to collect history you need to add a timestamp or snapshot date to every table in your model. Not only that but it needs to be in the primary key of the table so that you do not load duplicate rows on any given day. This of course complicates all the cascading foreign key (FK) relationships. In Figure 1 you can see a simple example of a standard Product and Product Category table with Snapshot Dates added to the keys.

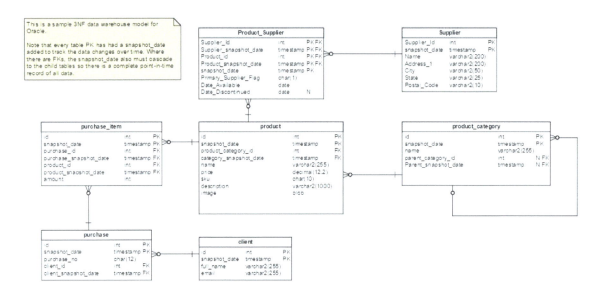

Even with this simple model you can start to see the issues. Adding a **snapshot date** to every PK makes all the keys more complicated. Imagine a master-detail-detail relationship with three levels of snapshot dates. This certainly will complicate not only your change data capture for loading the data warehouse but also your SQL to get the data out. How do you manage all those dates to get a current view of the data (let alone a specific point in time)? While this was a great approach to insure you had a full history of data, the resulting SQL becomes non-trivial to develop and maintain.

What if you missed a relationship in your initial modeling? Adding a new FK to this model would require reloading the table, and potentially losing any change history you had already captured.

Not agile.

Similarly in a **dimensional model**, it is not uncommon to get new requirements late in the game that causes you to rethink your design. For example, you have a sales fact table with the dimensions Customer, Product, and Supplier. You build the fact and the dims. Load the data from your source, aggregating by Customer, Product, and Supplier. Done.

Then you build a few reports or even prototype with a pivot table and the business realizes they forgot to say they need to do the analysis by Region and SalesPerson as well so they can calculate commissions. You now have two choices – build a new fact table or alter the existing fact table.

If you build a new fact table, you have to load the data from your source system, because the current fact table only has aggregated data. So now you have two load routines hitting the source for the same transactions. If you alter the existing fact table to add the FKs for the new dimensions, you have to reload that table from scratch (possibly losing history) because the current data is at the wrong grain.

Yes, there are solutions for these issues. People do this all the time. But it is **not agile**. Nor very forgiving of miss-steps.

Regardless of your skill, these type of issues become bigger and harder to handle **at scale**. Imagine your warehouse is hundreds of tables with millions or billions of rows. Refactoring and reloading tables at that scale will at least take a lot of time.

The Data Vault Modeling Method gives us an **Agile Data Engineering** approach to avoid these issues.

Formal Definition of Data Vault

This is the formal definition as written by the inventor Dan Linstedt (https://twitter.com/dlinstedt):

> The Data Vault (Model) is a detail oriented, historical tracking and uniquely linked set of normalized tables that support one or more functional areas of business.
>
> It is a hybrid approach encompassing the best of breed between 3rd normal form (3NF) and star schema. The design is flexible, scalable, consistent, and adaptable to the needs of the enterprise. It is a data model that is architected specifically to meet the needs of today's enterprise data warehouses.

The main point here is that Data Vault (DV) was developed *specifically* to address these and other issues in the data warehousing space. It was built to be a non-volatile, auditable, historical repository of enterprise data. (It does not however replace star schemas needed at the reporting layer – more on that later)

Foundational Keys to Data Vault

There are three key features found in the Data Vault approach that allow us to use it as an agile modeling technique. They are:

- Flexibility

- Productivity

- Scalability

As we go through this series of posts, I will show you how to model using Data Vault and how that approach allows us to achieve these three foundation goals.

Where Data Vault fits in the architecture

To be clear, there is nothing really new here. The Data Vault fits neatly where you see an **EDW** in most architecture diagrams. In Bill Inmon's Corporate Information Factory (CIF) approach, the DV fits right between the Stage layer and the Data Mart Layer. In a Kimball Bus Architecture, the DV becomes the Persistent Staging Area that feeds the Dimensional Data Warehouse.

So at a conceptual level, there is nothing new. It is rather the **modeling technique** (and the related loading paradigm) that are new (and much more suitable for agile).

Evolution of Data Vault Modeling

So how did we get here? Where did Data Vault come from?

Permit me for a moment to stroll down memory lane with regard to data modeling. Here is a brief timeline:

- 1960's:
  - E.F. Codd begins research on relational modeling (you know – 3NF and all that)
  - Dimension & Fact Modeling is developed by General Mills & Dartmouth University
- 1970's
  - E.F. Codd publishes "A Relational Model of Data for Large Shared Data Banks" - 1970
  - Bill Inmon introduces the idea of a Data Warehouse
  - AC Nielson popularizes the concepts of Facts and Dimensions
  - Dr. Peter Chen invents Entity Relationship Diagramming (ERDs) – 1976
- 1980's
  - Bill Inmon popularizes (and publishes) Data Warehousing
  - Dr. Ralph Kimball popularizes Star Schema design
  - Dr. Kimball and Barry Devlin release "Business Data Warehouse"
- 1990
  - Dan Linstedt begins R&D on Data Vault Modeling
- 2000
  - Dan Linstedt released the first 5 articles on Data Vault
- 2002
  - Dan starts giving public seminars on Data Vault
    - Yours truly signs up!
- 2008
  - Bill Inmon is quoted as supporting Data Vault as the method for his new DW 2.0 approach.
- 2014
  - Dan formally introduces Data Vault 2.0 at the 1st Annual World Wide Data Vault Consortium (WWDVC) in St Albans, Vermont to an international audience
- 2015

- 2nd Annual WWDVC is held in Stowe, Vermont

- 2016

  - 3rd Annual WWDVC will be held in Stowe, Vermont.

- 2019

  - 6th Annual WWDVC is held in Stow, Vermont (see wwdvc.com)

  - 1st Annual WWDVC Europe is held in Hanover, Germany

- 2021

  - 7th Annual WWDVC is held virtually due to COVID-19

  - DataVaultAlliance.com becomes the single source for DV 2.0 information

Who is using Data Vault?

Data Vault has been taught and in use around the world since 2002. Organizations you might know and some you don't have been using it for that long. Somewhere in the secret bowels of US Department of Defense (USDOD) it is used (but Dan can't say where). I set it up myself at Denver Public Schools, and used a hybrid of Data Vault 2.0 at McKesson Specialty Health (in Houston). A huge bank in Australia is using DV 2.0 and adding automation! In 2019, many large organizations, globally, have adopted DV 2.0, including chip manufacturers, commercial retailers, insurers, pharmas, and healthcare provivders.

Here is a short list of a few more notables:

- Paciolan

- Sainsbury's

- Pepsico

- Anthem Blue-Cross Blue Shield

- Finnair

- Independent Purchasing Cooperative (IPC, Miami) - Owner of Subway

Introducing Data Vault 2.0

Before I end, I wanted to give you a glimpse at what is new in Data Vault 2.0.

One of the notable features is that the modeling approach has been augmented to allow deploying parts of the Data Vault on a **Hadoop** or **NoSQL** engine (very cool). I will show you the specific changes for that in the next chapter.

But importantly, DV 2.0 is not just about the modeling. It also includes **best practices** for architecture, loading and methodology. The approach has been expanded to specifically include an agile method based on Scott Ambler's Disciplined Agile Development.

So Why Try Data Vault?

There is an old Chinese proverb:

> 'Unless you change direction, you're apt to end up where you're headed.'

So do you like where you are in your data warehouse practice today? Do you like where you are heading? Are you agile or agile-enough? ***Will you be successful?***

Chapter 2: Data Vault 2.0 Modeling Basics

The first part of this book, we looked at the need for an Agile Data Engineering solution, issues with some of the current data warehouse modeling approaches, the history of data modeling in general, and Data Vault specifically.

Now we get into the technical details of what the Data Vault Model looks like and how you build one.

For my examples I will be using a simple Human Resources (HR) type model that most people should relate to (even if you have never worked with an HR model). In this post I will walk through how you get from the OLTP model to the Data Vault model.

Data Vault Prime Directive

One thing to get very clear up front is that, unlike many data warehouse implementations today, the Data Vault **Method** requires that we load data **exactly** as it exists in the source system. No edits, no changes, no application of soft business rules (including data cleansing).

Why?

So that the Data Vault is 100% auditable.

If you alter the data on the way into the Data Vault, you break the ability to trace the data to the source in case of an audit because you cannot match the data warehouse data to source data. Remember your EDW (Enterprise Data Warehouse) is the **enterprise** store of **historical** data too. Once the data is purged from the source systems, your EDW may also be your **Source of Record**. So it is critical the data remain clean.

We have a saying in Data Vault world – The DV is a source of **FACTS**, not a source of TRUTH (truth is often subjective & relative in the data world).

Now, you **can** alter the data *downstream* from the Data Vault when you build your **Information Marts**. I will discuss that in more detail in the 3rd and 4th chapters.

Hubs

For a Data Vault, the first thing you do is model the Hubs. Hubs are the core of any DV design. If done properly, Hubs are what allow you to integrate multiple source systems in your data warehouse. To do that, they must be **source system agnostic**. That means they must be based on true **Business Keys** (or meaningful natural keys) that are **not** tied to any one source system.

That means you **should not** use source system surrogate keys for identification. Hubs keys must be based on an **identifiable business element** or elements.

What is an identifiable business element? It is a column (or set of columns) found in the systems that the business consistently uses to identify and locate the data. Regardless of source system, these elements must have the same **semantic** meaning (even though the names may vary from source to source). If you are very lucky, the source system model will have this defined for you in the form of **alternate unique keys or indexes**. If not you will need to engage in **data profiling** and conversations with the business customers to figure out what the business keys are.

This is the most important aspect of Data Vault modeling. You **must** get this right if you intend to build **an integrated enterprise data warehouse** for your organization.

(To be honest, in order to ***really, really*** do this **right**, you should start by building a conceptual model based on **business processes** using **business terminology**. If you do that, the Data Vault model will be most obvious to you and it will not be based on any existing source system).

As an example, look at these tables from a typical HR application. This is the source OLTP example we will work with:

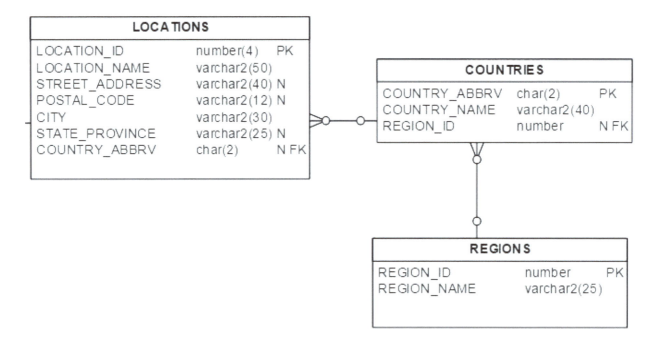

The Primary Key (PK) on the LOCATION table is LOCATION_ID. But that is an integer surrogate key. It is ***not a good candidate*** for the Business Key.

Why? Because **every** source system can have an ID of 1, 2, 201, 5389, etc. It is just a number and has **no meaning** in the real world. Instead LOCATION_NAME is the likely candidate for the Business Key (BK). Looking in the database, we see that it has a unique index. Great! (If there were no unique indexes, we would have to talk to the business and/or query the data directly to find a unique set of columns to use.)

For the COUNTRIES table, the COUNTRY_ABBRV column will work as a Business Key since it is the PK and therefore, we know it is unique. However, COUNTRY_NAME might be a candidate too if it is unique. If that is the case, the business users would have to tell us their preference. For REGIONS, the Business Key would likely be the REGION_NAME for the same reasons.

Fundamentally, a Hub is a **list of unique business keys**.

A Hub table has a very simple structure. It contains:

- A Hub PK

- The Business Key column(s)

- The Load Date (LOAD_DTS)

- The Source for the record (REC_SRC)

New in DV 2.0, the Hub PK is a **calculated** field consisting of a Hash (often MD5 or SHA1) of the Business Key columns (more on that in a bit).

The **Business Key** must be a declared unique or alternate key constraint in the Hub. That means for each key there will be only on row in the Hub table, ever. It can be a compound key made up of more than one column.

The **LOAD_DTS** tells us the **first** time the data warehouse "knew" about that business key. So no matter how many loads you run, this row is created the first time and never dropped or updated.

The **REC_SRC** tells us which source system the row came from. If the value can come from multiple sources, this will tell us which source fed us the value first.

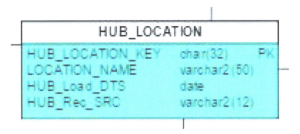

Figure 3 - Simple Hub Table

In the HUB_LOCATION table, LOCATION_NAME is the Business Key. It is a unique name used in the source systems to identify a location. It must have a unique constraint or index declared on it in the database to prevent duplicates from being entered and to facilitate faster query access.

What can you do with a single Hub table?

You can do data profiling and basic analysis on the business key. Answer questions like:

1. How many locations do we have?

2. How many source systems provide us locations names?

3. Are there data quality issues? Do we see Location Names that seem similar but are from different sources? (Hint: if you do, you may have a **master data management issue**)

Hash-based Primary Keys

One of the **innovations** in DV 2.0 was the replacement of the standard integer surrogate keys with hash-based primary keys. This was to allow a DV solution to be deployed, at least in part, on a **Hadoop** solution. Hadoop systems do not have surrogate key generators like a modern RDBMS, but you can generate an MD5 Hash. With a Hash Key in Hadoop and one in your RDBMS, you can "logically" join this data (with the right tools of course). Plus, sequence generators and counters can become a bottleneck on some database systems at very high volumes and degrees of parallelism.

Here is an example of Oracle code to create the HUB_LOCATION_KEY:

dbms_obfuscation_toolkit.md5(upper(trim(nvl(LOCATION_NAME,''))))

In Snowflake, the code is even simpler:

md5(upper(trim(nvl(LOCATION_NAME,''))))

For a Hub and source Stage tables, we apply an MD5 (or SHA1 or SHA2) hash calculation to the Business Key columns. If you have so much data coming so fast that you cannot load it quickly into your database, one option is to build stage tables (really copies of source tables) on Hadoop, or in blob storage in the cloud (e.g. AWS S3) so you do not lose the data. As you load those files, the hash calculation is applied to the Business Key and added as a new piece of data during the load. Then when it is time to load to your database you can compare the Hash Key in your "data lake" to the Hash Key in your Hub table to see if the data is loaded already or not. (Note: how to load a data vault is too much for this little ebook to cover; please look at the Data Vault book on amazon.com, Building a Scalable Data Warehouse Using Data Vault 2.0 or sign up for a Data Vault 2.0 Bootcamp class to learn more. Check out DataVaultAlliance.com for details on training.

Links

The Link is the key to **flexibility** and **scalability** in the Data Vault modeling technique. They are modeled in such a way as to allow for changes and additions to the model over time by providing the ability to easily add new objects and relationships **without** having to change existing structures or load routines.

In a Data Vault model, all source data relationships (i.e., foreign keys) and events are represented as Links. One of the foundational rules in DV is that Hubs can have no FKs, so to represent the joins between Hub concepts, we must use a Link table. The purpose of the Link is to capture and record the relationship of data elements at the lowest possible grain. Other examples of Links include transactions and hierarchies (because in reality those are the intersection of a bunch of Hubs too).

A Link is therefore an **intersection** of business keys. It contains the columns that represent the business keys from the related Hubs. A Link **must** have more than one parent table. There must be a **least** two Hubs, but, as in the case of a transaction, they may be composed of many Hubs. A Link table's grain is defined by the number of parent keys it contains (very similar to a Fact table in dimensional modeling).

Like a Hub, the Link is also technically a simple structure. It contains:

- A Link PK (Hash Key)

- The PKs from the parent Hubs – used for lookups

- The Business Key column(s) – **new feature in DV 2.0**

- The Load Date (LOAD_DTS)

- The Source for the record (REC_SRC)

Figure 4 Link and Parent Hubs

In Figure 4 you see the results of converting the FK to REGIONS from the COUNTRIES table (Figure 2) into a Link table. The PK column LNK_REGION_COUNTRY_KEY is a hash key calculated against the Business Key columns from the contributing Hubs. This gives us a unique key for every combination of Country and Region that may be fed to us by the source systems.

In Oracle that might look like:

***dbms_obfuscation_toolkit.md5(upper(trim(nvl(COUNTRY_ABBRV,''))||'^'||
upper(trim(nvl(REGION_NAME,''))))***

Just as in the Hubs, the Link records only the **first time** that the relationship appears in the DV.

In addition, the Link contains the PKs from the parent Hubs (which should be declared as an alternate unique key or index). This makes up the natural key for the Link.

New to DV 2.0 is the inclusion of the text business key columns from the parent Hubs. Yes, this is a specific de-normalization. It is optional.

Why? For query performance when you want to extract data from the Data Vault (more on in later chapters). Depending on your platform, you may consider adding a unique key constraint or index on these columns as well.

Why are Links Many-to-Many?

Links are intersection tables and so, by design, they represent a many-to-many relationship. Since a FK is usually 1:M, you may ask why it is done this way.

One word: **Flexibility**!

Remember that part of the goal of the Data Vault is to store only the **facts** and **avoid** reengineering (refactoring) even if the business rules or source systems change. So if you did your business modeling right, the only thing that might change would be the cardinality of a relationship. Now granted it is not likely that one Region will ever be in two Countries, but if that rule changed or you get a new source system that allows it, the 1:M might become a M:M. With a Link, we can handle either with *no change to the design or the load process*!

That is **dynamic** adaptability. That is an **agile** design. (Maximize the amount of work **not** done.)

Using this type of design pattern allows us to more quickly adapt and absorb business rule and source system changes while minimizing the need to re-engineer the Data Vault. Less work. Less time. No re-testing. Less money!

Satellites

Satellites (or **Sats** for short) are where all the big action is in a Data Vault. These structures are where all the **descriptive** (i.e., non-key) columns go, plus this is where the Change Data Capture (**CDC**) is done and **history** is stored. The structure and concept are very much like a Type 2 Slowly Changing Dimension.

To accomplish this function, the Primary Key for a Sat contains two parts: the PK from its Parent Hub (or Link) plus the LOAD_DTS. So every time we load the DV and find new records or changed records, we insert those records into the Sats and give them a timestamp. (On a side note, this structure also means that a DV is real-time-ready in that you can load whenever and as often as you need as long as you set the LOAD_DTS correctly.)

This is the only structure in the core Data Vault that has a two-part key. That is as complicated as it gets from a structure perspective.

Of course, a Sat must also have the REC_SRC column for auditability. REC_SRC will tell us the source of each row of data in the Sat.

Important Note: The REC_SRC in a Sat does **NOT** have to be the same as that in the parent Hub or Link. Remember that Hubs and Links record the source of the concept key or relationship the **first** time the DV sees it. Subsequent loads may find **different** sources provide **different** descriptive information at different times for one single Hub record (don't forget that we are **integrating** systems too).

You may have noticed that not all the columns in **Figure 1** ended up in the Hubs or the Link tables that we have looked at.

Where do they go? They go in the Sats.

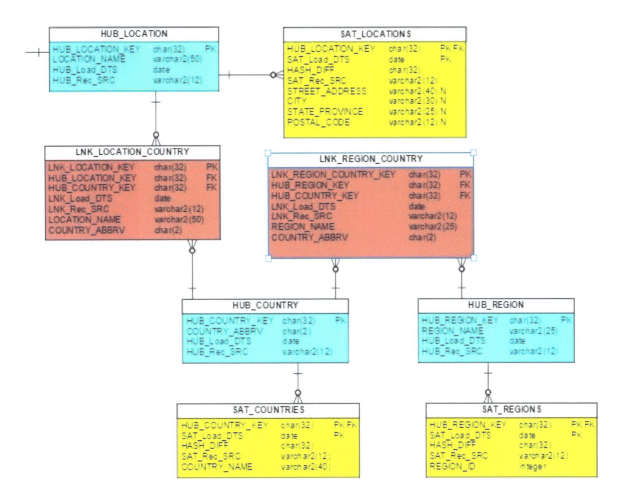

Figure 5 Hubs and Links with Sats

In Figure 5, look at SAT_LOCATIONS. There you see all the address columns from the original table LOCATIONS (Figure 2). Likewise in SAT_COUNTRIES you see COUNTRY_NAME and in SAT_REGIONS you see REGION_ID (remember that was the source system PK but NOT the Business Key, so it goes here so we can trace back to the source if needed).

Use of HASH_DIFF columns for Change Data Capture (CDC)

Another **innovation** that came with **DV 2.0** is the use of a Hash-based column for determining if a record in the source has changed from what was previously loaded into the Data Vault. We call that a Hash Diff (for **diff**erence). Every Sat must have this column to be DV 2.0 compliant.

So, how this works is that you first calculate a Hash on the combination of **all** of the descriptive (non-meta data) columns in the Sat.

Examples for Oracle for the three Sats in Figure 5 are:

SAT_REGIONS.HASH_DIFF = dbms_obfuscation_toolkit.md5(to_char(nvl(REGION_ID,'')))

SAT_COUNTRIES.HASH_DIFF = dbms_obfuscation_toolkit.md5(trim(nvl(COUNTRY_NAME,'')))

SAT_LOCATIONS.HASH_DIFF =
dbms_obfuscation_toolkit.md5(trim(nvl(STREET_ADDRESS,''))||'^'||trim(nvl(CITY,''))||^||trim(nvl(ST ATE_PROVINCE,''))||'^'||trim(POSTAL_CODE))

Now when you get ready to do another load, you must calculate a Hash on the inbound values (using **exactly** the same formula) and then compare that to the HASH_DIFF column in the Sat for the most recent row (i.e., from the last load date) for the **same** Hub Business Key. If the Hash calculation is different, then you create a new row. If not, you do nothing (which is way faster).

This is **exactly** what you do when you build a Type 2 SCD (*Slowly Changing Dimension*).

The **difference** is that instead of comparing every single column in the feed to every single column in the Sat, you only have to compare one column – the HASH_DIFF. (See my *white paper Using Decode for Change Data Capture* on **kentgraziano.com** to learn on how we did it in DV 1.0)

So which do you think is **faster** on a very wide table?

Comparing **one** column vs. **50** columns (or several hundred columns)?

In fact, since all the HASH_DIFFs are the **same size**, the speed of the comparison allows you to **scale** to wider tables without the CDC process slowing your down.

Is it overkill for a small, narrow table? Probably.

But if you want a **standards** based, **repeatable** approach, you apply the same rules regardless. Plus if you follow the **patterns**, you can automate the generation of the design and load processes (or buy software that does it for you).

Another Note: *There are no updates! We never over write data in a Data Vault! We only insert new data. That allows us to keep a clean audit trail.*

Summary

So there you have the basics (and then some) of what makes up a raw Data Vault Data Model and you have seen some of the innovations from Data Vault 2.0

Just remember this list:

- Hubs = Business Keys

- Links = Associations / Transactions

- Satellites = Descriptors

Hubs make it **business driven** and allow for **integration** across systems

Links give you the **flexibility** to absorb structural and business rule changes without re-engineering (and therefore without reloading any data).

Sats give you the **adaptability** to record history at any interval you want plus unquestionable **auditability** and **traceability** to your source systems.

All together you get agility, flexibility, adaptability, auditability, scalability, and **speed to market**.

What more could a data warehouse architect want?

Want more in-depth details about the Data Vault? Check out the Data Vault 2.0 book, Building a Scalable Data Warehouse with Data Vault 2.0.

Ready to learn how to **load** Hubs, Links, and Satellites? Then check out some online training available at DataVaultAlliance.com/classes to learn how to load the Data Vault.

As a special for my readers, you can use the coupon code **AgileDW10** to get 10% off anything on that site.

Chapter 3: The Business Data Vault

In the last chapter, we looked at the basics of modeling your data warehouse using the Data Vault 2.0 technique.

In this chapter we get into the details of how we **prepare** the DV tables for business user access.

What is a Business Data Vault?

If you have done any investigation into Data Vault on various blogs or the LinkedIn discussion group, you have seen a few terms used that often cause confusion. These terms include:

- Business Vault

- Information Vault

- Business Data Vault

- Raw Vault

- Raw Data Vault

So first off, we need to say that from a terminology perspective:

Business Vault = Business Data Vault = Information Vault

And

Raw Vault = Raw Data Vault = Data Vault = The Vault

When the majority of people say "Data Vault," they are referring to what we now may call a Raw Vault. Prior to the addition of the Business Vault, the Raw Vault was universally called the Data Vault, the term "**raw**" was added so we could be clear on which part of the architecture we were discussing.

What is a **Raw Vault**? It is what I described in the last chapter – it is the raw, unfiltered data from the source, loaded into Hubs, Links, and Satellites based on Business Keys.

Now for the definition of a Business Vault (**BV**): It is an **extension** of a Raw Vault that applies **selected business rules**, denormalizations, calculations, and other query assistance functions in order to **facilitate** user access and reporting. Business Vault tables should be refreshed once their **dependent** Raw Vault tables are refreshed.

Some more details about what a Business Vault is…

It is first off modeled in DV Style tables (that is Hubs, Links, and Sats), but it is **not a complete copy** of all the objects in the Raw Vault. It is selective in that we create only structures that hold some **significant business value**. In this case I mean we will **transform** the data in some way to apply rules or functions that most of the business users will find useful (as opposed to doing these repeatedly into multiple marts). This includes things like **data cleansing**, **data quality**, **accounting rules**, or **well-defined repeatable calculations** (e.g., net profit, total compensation, etc.).

Adding Business Vault tables is an **option** to the Raw Vault. It is **not required**. You can have a perfectly compliant Data Vault without one. As usually it **depends** on the business and reporting requirements you have to fulfill.

The **primary** group to use or access the BV is your **power users**. These are people who understand SQL and relational models well and are not afraid of having many table joins. They may need to do some exploration or data mining but either do not want to wait for the star schemas to be built or are not doing dimensional analysis (remember the BV is Data Vault style table and joins!). **The majority of your users should *not*** be given access to this layer of the architecture, rather they should be querying the data via the Information Mart layer (more on that in the next chapter), or via a Business Intelligence tool.

As of Data Vault 2.0, the Business Vault also includes some specialty tables that help us in building more efficient queries against the Raw Vault. These are Point-in-Time (PIT) tables and Bridge Tables.

PIT Tables

A Point-in-Time (PIT) table is a modified Satellite that helps when we need to query data from a Hub that has multiple Satellites.

Take for example, this Employee Hub which has four Satellites:

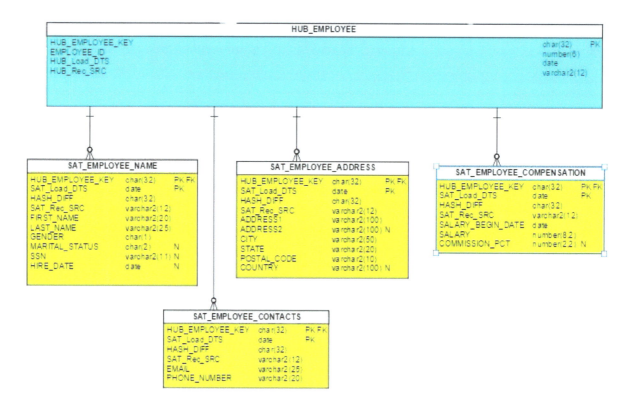

Figure 6 Hub with Multiple Sats

NB: *It was pointed out to me that one Sat in Figure 6 is named plural (CONTACTS) and the others are singular. That was an oversight on my part – I did not apply a good naming standard! Pick one – singular or plural, and try to stick with it.*

A Hub can have multiple Sats for several reasons:

1. There are multiple source systems with different attributes coming from each source

2. There are specific data classifications that you want to split out

3. The rate of change of certain attributes if faster/slower than others

4. Combinations of the above

In the example in Figure 6, you see four Sats with different types of data: Name (and other basic demographics), Address, Compensation, and Contacts. Now while they may each be coming from different source systems, we can't really tell with the information we have. However we can guess that an employee's address probably changes more often than their name, and hopefully their compensation more often than that! The same may be true for an employee's contact information.

Why split on **rate of change**? Simple math. Every time a value changes on one attribute on a row, we have to load the entire row into the Sat. If one attributes changes 100 times, we load 100 rows. So even of the rest of the attributes did not change, we still have to load that data. This can cause an explosion in size for a large Sat with a few rapidly changing attributes. (Note – this is not as big a concern if you are using a database like Snowflake that uses column compression.)

So by separating these attributes out by rate of change, we help reduce the overall disk storage required for the Hub. And query performance for those Sats will be better if there are fewer rows (at least on most databases).

With multiple Sats being loaded independently (based on when the data changes), we now need to figure out how we get the data out of the Raw Vault and get a result that is **consistent across time**. This will usually require some form of **nested sub query**. Even to get the most current set of values will require something like this:

```
SELECT H.HUB_EMPLOYEE_KEY, H.EMPLOYEE_ID, S.FIRST_NAME, S.LAST_NAME, S.HIRE_DATE

FROM HUB_EMPLOYEE H

JOIN SAT_EMPLOYEE_NAME S

ON H. HUB_EMPLOYEE_KEY = S. HUB_EMPLOYEE_KEY

WHERE S.SAT_LOAD_DTS =

(SELECT MAX(S2.SAT_LOAD_DTS)

FROM SAT_EMPLOYEE_NAME S2

WHERE H. HUB_EMPLOYEE_KEY = S2. HUB_EMPLOYEE_KEY)
```

If we want to include data from one of the other Sats, the query gets a bit more complex:

```
SELECT H.HUB_EMPLOYEE_KEY, H.EMPLOYEE_ID, S.FIRST_NAME, S.LAST_NAME, S.HIRE_DATE, C.SALARY

FROM HUB_EMPLOYEE H

JOIN SAT_EMPLOYEE_NAME S

ON H. HUB_EMPLOYEE_KEY = S. HUB_EMPLOYEE_KEY

WHERE S.SAT_LOAD_DTS =

(SELECT MAX(S2.SAT_LOAD_DTS)

FROM SAT_EMPLOYEE_NAME S2

WHERE H. HUB_EMPLOYEE_KEY = S2. HUB_EMPLOYEE_KEY)

JOIN SAT_EMPLOYEE_COMPENSATION C

ON H. HUB_EMPLOYEE_KEY = C. HUB_EMPLOYEE_KEY
```

> **WHERE C.SAT_LOAD_DTS =**
>
> **(SELECT MAX(S3.SAT_LOAD_DTS)**
>
> **FROM SAT_EMPLOYEE_NAME S3**
>
> **WHERE H. HUB_EMPLOYEE_KEY = S3. HUB_EMPLOYEE_KEY)**

And so on... (you need additional clauses for **every** additional Sat table accessed)

Now imagine you need not the current view of the data, but a picture of the **historical** data from a point-in-time. After all this is a data warehouse, right!

You now need to **align** the various load dates so you get the row from each Sat that was valid during a specific time period or on a specific date. The SQL now gets longer and more complicated; beyond the abilities of many SQL people. They query now looks like this:

> SELECT H.HUB_EMPLOYEE_KEY, H.EMPLOYEE_ID, S.FIRST_NAME, S.LAST_NAME, S.HIRE_DATE**,**
> **C.SALARY**
>
> FROM HUB_EMPLOYEE H
>
> JOIN SAT_EMPLOYEE_NAME S
>
> ON H. HUB_EMPLOYEE_KEY = S. HUB_EMPLOYEE_KEY
>
> WHERE S.SAT_LOAD_DTS =
>
> (SELECT MAX(S2.SAT_LOAD_DTS)
>
> FROM SAT_EMPLOYEE_NAME S2
>
> WHERE H. HUB_EMPLOYEE_KEY = S2. HUB_EMPLOYEE_KEY
>
> **AND S2.SAT_LOAD_DTS < '25-Nov-2014')**
>
> JOIN SAT_EMPLOYEE_COMPENSATION C
>
> ON H. HUB_EMPLOYEE_KEY = C. HUB_EMPLOYEE_KEY
>
> WHERE C.SAT_LOAD_DTS =
>
> (SELECT MAX(S3.SAT_LOAD_DTS)
>
> FROM SAT_EMPLOYEE_NAME S3
>
> WHERE H. HUB_EMPLOYEE_KEY = S3. HUB_EMPLOYEE_KEY
>
> **AND S2.SAT_LOAD_DTS < '25-Nov-2014')**
>
> ...

(Note: this is why it is said that the Raw Vault is **NOT** for end user query – it is for efficiently storing the historical data.)

Hence the need for the Business Vault feature called the PIT table.

The PIT table will help us **simplify** the query by doing the load date alignment for us. The PIT table is **loaded after** or along with the Raw Vault (once it's **dependent** RV tables are loaded of course). In Figure 7, there is now an EMPLOYEE_PIT table.

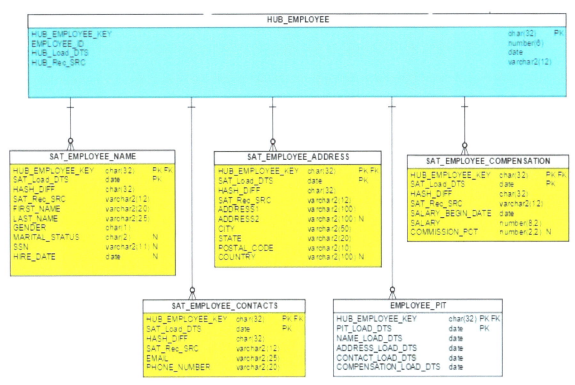

TIP: Technically speaking, the PIT table is part of the BV while the rest of the tables are in the Raw Vault. From an implementation perspective, they can (and probably should) live in the same schema.

Here now is an example of what the data in this PIT table might look like:

HUB_EMPLOYEE_KEY	PIT_LOAD_DTS	NAME_LOAD_DTS	ADDRESS_LOAD_DTS	CONTACT_LOAD_DTS	COMPENSATION_LOAD_DTS
157F442NMQQ92S	01-Jan-2014	01-Jan-2014	NULL	NULL	NULL
157F442NMQQ92S	02-Jan-2014	01-Jan-2014	02-Jan-2014	NULL	02-Jan-2014
157F442NMQQ92S	03-Jan-2014	01-Jan-2014	02-Jan-2014	03-Jan-2014	03-Jan-2014
...					
157F442NMQQ92S	15-Feb-2015	24-Jun-2014	30-Jul-2014	10-Jan-2015	31-Dec-2014

So now if we need to get a picture of the data as it was on February 15, 2015, we simply join to the PIT table to find which load dates to use.

```
SELECT H.HUB_EMPLOYEE_KEY, H.EMPLOYEE_ID, S.FIRST_NAME, S.LAST_NAME, S.HIRE_DATE,
C.SALARY, …

FROM HUB_EMPLOYEE H

JOIN SAT_EMPLOYEE_NAME NM

ON H. HUB_EMPLOYEE_KEY = NM. HUB_EMPLOYEE_KEY

JOIN SAT_EMPLOYEE_COMPENSATION COMP

ON H. HUB_EMPLOYEE_KEY = COMP. HUB_EMPLOYEE_KEY

JOIN SAT_EMPLOYEE_ADDRESS ADDR

ON H. HUB_EMPLOYEE_KEY = ADDR. HUB_EMPLOYEE_KEY

JOIN SAT_EMPLOYEE_CONTACTS CNTC

ON H. HUB_EMPLOYEE_KEY = CNTC. HUB_EMPLOYEE_KEY

JOIN EMPLOYEE_PIT P

ON H. HUB_EMPLOYEE_KEY = P. HUB_EMPLOYEE_KEY

AND P.PIT_LOAD_DTS = '15-FEB-2015'

AND P.NAME_LOAD_DTS = NM.SAT_LOAD_DTS

AND P.ADDRESS_LOAD_DTS = ADDR.SAT_LOAD_DTS

AND P.CONTACT_LOAD_DTS = CNTC.SAT_LOAD_DTS

AND P.COMPENSATION_LOAD_DTS = COMP.SAT_LOAD_DTS
```

So, if you are loading the PIT table every day, with no gaps, no more subqueries and no more MAX(LOAD_DTS) clauses. This is much **easier to read, understand, and tune**! (Yes – you should add outer joins if the some of the dates in the PIT will be NULL.)

If there are gaps in the load dates of the PIT tables, then the query does need a modification to add one subquery:

```
SELECT H.HUB_EMPLOYEE_KEY, H.EMPLOYEE_ID, S.FIRST_NAME, S.LAST_NAME, S.HIRE_DATE,
C.SALARY, …

FROM HUB_EMPLOYEE H

JOIN SAT_EMPLOYEE_NAME NM

ON H. HUB_EMPLOYEE_KEY = NM. HUB_EMPLOYEE_KEY

JOIN SAT_EMPLOYEE_COMPENSATION COMP
```

ON H. HUB_EMPLOYEE_KEY = COMP. HUB_EMPLOYEE_KEY

JOIN SAT_EMPLOYEE_ADDRESS ADDR

ON H. HUB_EMPLOYEE_KEY = ADDR. HUB_EMPLOYEE_KEY

JOIN SAT_EMPLOYEE_CONTACTS CNTC

ON H. HUB_EMPLOYEE_KEY = CNTC. HUB_EMPLOYEE_KEY

JOIN EMPLOYEE_PIT P

ON H. HUB_EMPLOYEE_KEY = P. HUB_EMPLOYEE_KEY

AND P.PIT_LOAD_DTS =

(SELECT MAX(P2.PIT_LOAD_DTS)

FROM EMPLOYEE_PIT P2

WHERE H. HUB_EMPLOYEE_KEY = P2. HUB_EMPLOYEE_KEY

AND P2.PIT_LOAD_DTS <= '15-FEB-2015')

AND P.NAME_LOAD_DTS = NM.SAT_LOAD_DTS

AND P.ADDRESS_LOAD_DTS = ADDR.SAT_LOAD_DTS

AND P.CONTACT_LOAD_DTS = CNTC.SAT_LOAD_DTS

AND P.COMPENSATION_LOAD_DTS = COMP.SAT_LOAD_DTS

Even though we need a subquery, one subquery will process faster than the four subqueries needed if there is no PIT table.

Bridge Tables

Like a Point-in-Time table, a Bridge table also makes it easier to query the Data Vault and helps performance at the same time by reducing the number of hops through the model. In the case of a Bridge table, it is used to simplify joins that involve multiple Hubs and Links. It is really a **derived** Link table (linking multiple Hubs and Links together) that supports answering a particular set of questions.

As you will see, some of the potential query performance improvements will come by simply reducing the number of tables required to get the answer we are looking for. As an example, using our HR data vault model (figure 8), suppose you wanted to get the full address of a LOCATION with its COUNTRY and REGION.

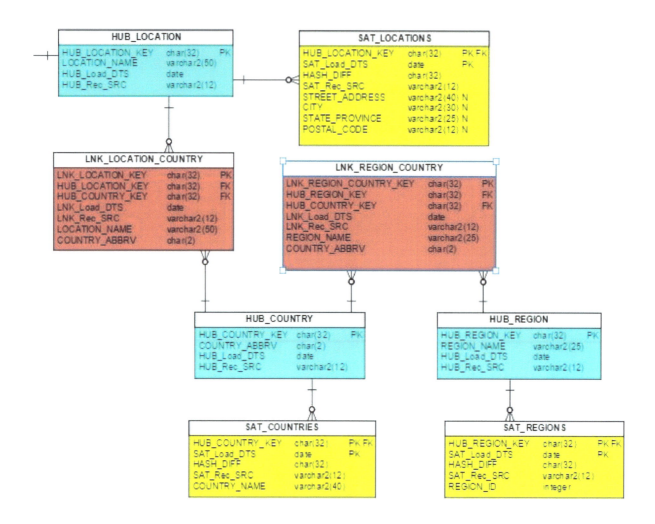

Figure 8 Location Geography

The query requires an eight (8) table join to get all the data elements required:

> SELECT H1.LOCATION_NAME, S1.STREET_ADDRESS, S1.CITY, S1.STATE_PROVINCE, S1.POSTAL_CODE, S2.COUNTRY_NAME, H3.REGION_NAME, S3.REGION_ID
>
> FROM **HUB_LOCATION** H1
>
> JOIN **SAT_LOCATIONS** S1
>
> ON H1.HUB_LOCATION_KEY = S1.HUB_LOCATION_KEY
>
> JOIN **LNK_LOCATION_COUNTRY** L1
>
> ON H1.HUB_LOCATION_KEY = L1.HUB_LOCATION_KEY
>
> JOIN **HUB_COUNTRY** H2
>
> ON L1.HUB_COUNTRY_KEY = H2.HUB_COUNTRY_KEY
>
> JOIN **SAT_COUNTRIES** S2

ON H2.HUB_COUNTRY_KEY = S2.HUB_COUNTRY_KEY

JOIN **LNK_REGION_COUNTRY** L2

ON H2.HUB_COUNTRY_KEY = L2.HUB_COUNTRY_KEY

JOIN **HUB_REGION** H3

ON L2.HUB_REGION_KEY = H3.HUB_REGION_KEY

JOIN **SAT_REGIONS** S3

ON H3.HUB_REGION_KEY = S3.HUB_REGION_KEY

To **improve** (or simplify) this query (which is one the business may need on a regular basis), we can build a Bridge table in the Business Vault. The Bridge table will hold **all** the keys needed to get all the data from the right Satellites **plus** the text Business Keys for the Hubs (as they are often needed in the queries too).

(**Note** in Figure 9, I have added 3 *invalid* FK lines between the Sats and the Bridge in order to simply illustrate the new *join* path. I had to "fake" it in the tool so the Bridge PK did not inherit down)

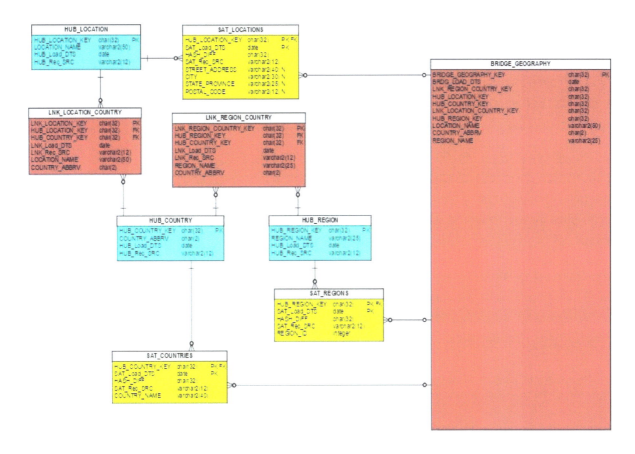

Figure 9 Geographic Bridge Table

By adding a derived Bridge table, we can do the same query now with only four (4) tables.

```
SELECT BRDG.LOCATION_NAME, S1.STREET_ADDRESS, S1.CITY, S1.STATE_PROVINCE,
S1.POSTAL_CODE, S2.COUNTRY_NAME, BRDG.REGION_NAME, S3.REGION_ID

FROM BRIDGE_GEOGRAPHY BRDG

JOIN SAT_LOCATIONS S1

ON BRDG.HUB_LOCATION_KEY = S1.HUB_LOCATION_KEY

JOIN SAT_COUNTRIES S2

ON BRDG.HUB_COUNTRY_KEY = S2.HUB_COUNTRY_KEY

JOIN SAT_REGIONS S3

ON BRDG.HUB_REGION_KEY = S3.HUB_REGION_KEY
```

To truly complete this picture, you may want to add a PIT table on the BRIDGE_GEOGRAPHY to record the LOAD_DTS changes in the three associated Sats.

Bridge Tables in DV 2.0

With the addition of the denormalized text Business Keys in the Link tables (mentioned in the previous chapter), Link tables now look much like the Bridge table. Notice in LNK_COUNTRY_LOCATION that LOCATION_NAME and COUNTRY_ABBR are in the table along with the Hub Keys. That means in **simple** cases, *you can use the Link as a Bridge table*.

If you are joining across multiple Links and even to Satellites on Links, you may still want to build a Bridge table to help with the query. As with many things in data warehousing, *it depends* on your reporting requirements and the complexity of the resulting query.

Add Bridge tables to your Business Vault **only** after you have determined you have a query performance issue as there is a cost here. While a Bridge does make the query much simpler to understand, and hopefully more performant, you now need a process to populate the Bridge table. So, there is a balance here – does the improvement in the query response offset the cost and time required to populate the Bridge?

Predefined Derivations

There is one other main category of objects that you may need to add to your Business Vault – tables containing predefined calculations or derivations. These tables should be structured to look like Links or Sats attached to existing Hubs or Links in the Raw Vault.

One of the goals for **flexibility** in the Data Vault architecture is to be able to build and re-build Information Marts quickly and also to ensure that the data in multiple marts is **consistently calculated**.

So in the case of derivations or calculations that will be used by many people in many contexts, it is often best to define that data **once** in the Business Vault then source the Information Marts from there.

As an example, imagine the HR department wants to be able to quickly report the minimum, maximum, and average annual salary, and total compensation to date of an employee over their entire history with the company. To make sure that these are calculated the same in every mart, we might add a salary summary Satellite to HUB_EMPLOYEE.

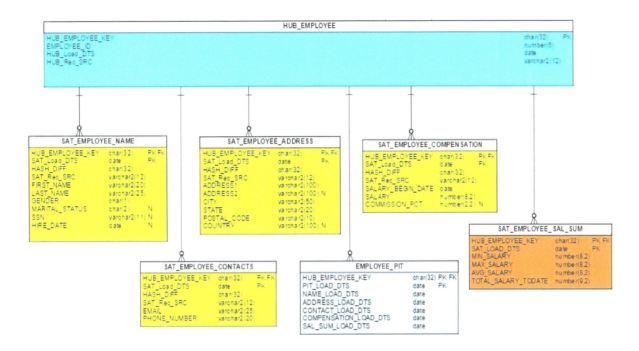

Figure 10 Hub Employee with Derived Satellite

In Figure 10, you can see I added a new Sat called SAT_EMPLOYEE_SAL_SUM. It contains **calculated** columns MIN_SALARY, MAX_SALARY, AVG_SALARY, and TOTAL_SALARY_TODATE. The SAT_LOAD_DTS column will tell us when the calculation was last run. No HASH_DIFF column or REC_SRC column are needed because this table contains calculated data and is populated on demand.

It is up to you and the business requirements as to how often you rerun the aggregation. It may be wise to trigger the re-aggregation anytime SAT_EMPLOYEE_COMPENSATION is updated for a particular employee, or maybe just run it once a quarter?

Again, since this is a **Business Vault** feature, it should be **driven** by the **business requirements**.

Notice also that I added **SUM_SAL_LOAD_DTS** to the **EMPLOYEE_PIT** table. This will make it easier to query the employees current NAME, SALARY, and other information alongside the summary information.

TIP: When you add new Satellites to your Raw Vault, be sure to check for PIT tables that need updating as well.

In the next chapter, I will show you how we use the Raw Vault and the Business Vault to build Information Marts.

Chapter 4: Building an Information Mart

In this last chapter of our introduction to Data Vault 2.0, we looked at how we prepare data for use with a concept called the Business Data Vault.

In this final chapter I will show you the basics of how we **project** the Business Vault and Raw DV tables into star schemas which form the basis for our Information Marts.

Raw Data Mart vs Information Marts

As of Data Vault 2.0, the terminology changed a bit to be more precise. With DV 2.0 we now speak of "**Information Marts**" rather than just "Data Marts".

Why?

Because truly when we build a star schema (or any style reporting table) on top of the DV, it usually involves some level of translation, transformation, or application of soft business rules (ala Business Vault). As such, our goal is to turn **data** into **information** that is useful for making business decisions.

On the other hand we also speak of what are best called **Raw Data Marts**. These are structures built on top of the Raw Data Vault by simply joining some of the DV tables together. The Raw Data Mart is an excellent option for **agile data warehouse projects**. I have used these on many occasions to get the **raw, uncleansed**, source data in front of the business users early on in a project. Confronted with the true (and often ugly) nature of their source data, I find that many business users find it much easier to then articulate the real business rules they need applied for the final reports (i.e., Information Marts).

In the next sections I will show you how to build Facts and Dimensions for both a Raw Mart and an Information Mart.

Dimensions

The simplest dimension is easily built by **joining** of a Hub and a Satellite. First you must decide if you need a Type 1 or a Type 2 dimension.

Type 1 Dimension for a Raw Data Mart

For a **Type 1**, which shows the most **current** values for all the attributes, we can use the Hub Key as the surrogate primary key (PK) for the dimension. I suggest using the **existing Hub Key** (the MD5 hash column) as it is already **unique** and will **save** you the processing of generating a typical integer surrogate for the dimension. This will save you processing time and allow you to load fact tables **before** or in parallel with the dimension. All the other columns in a Dimension will come from the contributing Hub and Satellite.

In the case of wanting to build a dimension for **Countries**, the following SQL can be used for a Type 1 Country Dimension:

```
SELECT
```

```sql
HC.HUB_COUNTRY_KEY AS DIM1_COUNTRY_KEY,

HC.COUNTRY_ABBRV,

SC.COUNTRY_NAME,

SC.SAT_Load_DTS AS EFFECTIVE_DTS,

SC.SAT_Rec_SRC  AS REC_SRC
FROM
HUB_COUNTRY HC, SAT_COUNTRIES SC
WHERE HC.HUB_COUNTRY_KEY = SC.HUB_COUNTRY_KEY

AND SC.SAT_Load_DTS =

        (

          SELECT

            MAX(S2.SAT_Load_DTS)

          FROM

            SAT_COUNTRIES S2

          WHERE

            HC.HUB_COUNTRY_KEY = S2.HUB_COUNTRY_KEY

        )
```

As you can see, I renamed the Hub Key to be DIM1_COUNTRY_KEY. DIM1 indicating this is a Type1 slowly changing dimension. For "as-of" date, I have aliased the Sat Load Date to be called EFFECTIVE_DTS. Then to insure we are only looking at the current values for every Country, I included a Max(Load Date) type subquery on the Load Date.

In Figure 11 you can see the Raw Vault model side-by-side with the projected Type 1 Dimension.

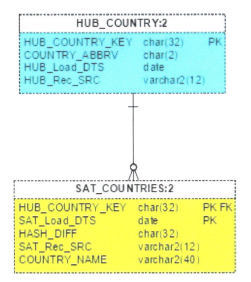 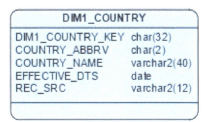

Figure 11 Projecting a Type 1 Dimension from a Raw Vault

For implementation, you simply build the dimension table, and then load it using the SQL code shown above.

Type 2 Dimension for a Raw Data Mart

Projecting a Type 2 slowly changing dimension (SCD) is only slightly more difficult. Since a Type 2 tracks changes to values over time (just like a Satellite), that means there may be **more than one** row in the Dimension for each business key (in this case COUNTRY_ABBRV). Because of that, you cannot use the Hub Key as the primary key on the Dimension.

If you are using DV 2.0, then I suggest you create the surrogate PK by using the same MD5 hash approach as we did in the Raw Vault. So to get a unique key in this case, you need to create a hash based on the Business Key **plus** the SAT_LOAD_DTS.

For Snowflake the Hash looks like this: **MD5(upper(trim(HC.COUNTRY_ABBRV)) || '^' || TO_CHAR(SC.SAT_Load_DTS, 'YYYY-MM-DD'))**

The entire query to build a Type 2 SCD for Country looks like this:

```
SELECT
  md5(upper(trim(nvl(HC.COUNTRY_ABBRV,''))))
  || '^'
  || TO_CHAR(SC.SAT_Load_DTS, 'YYYY-MM-DD')) AS DIM2_COUNTRY_KEY,
  HC.COUNTRY_ABBRV,
```

```
        SC.COUNTRY_NAME,

        SC.SAT_Load_DTS AS EFFECTIVE_DTS,

        LEAD(SC.SAT_Load_DTS)

                OVER (PARTITION BY SC.HUB_COUNTRY_KEY

                ORDER BY  SC.SAT_Load_DTS) AS EXPIRE_DTS,

        SC.SAT_Rec_SRC AS REC_SRC

    FROM

        HUB_COUNTRY HC,

        SAT_COUNTRIES SC

    WHERE

        HC.HUB_COUNTRY_KEY = SC.HUB_COUNTRY_KEY
```

Since this is a Type2, in addition to wanting to see an **effective** date (like in the Type 1), most users also need either an **Expiration Date** or a Current Flag so they can easily report on current or historical values. In this example I chose to create an EXPIRE_DTS field using the SQL analytic function **LEAD**. (If you have not used this function, basically it grabs the SAT_Load_DTS value from the next row for the same key. So if there is no next row, then the Expire Date will be NULL.)

With this method a user (or report) can see the current rows by using the clause **WHERE EXPIRE_DTS IS NULL**.

Figure 12 displays the resulting model.

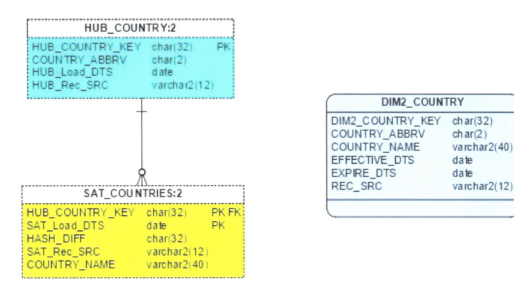

Type 1 Dimension for an Information Mart

This is very similar in structure and code as the Type 1 for the Raw Mart. The only difference is that the Dimension is built using tables that may be in the Raw Vault and in the Business Vault. For the example, I will show you a dimension for Employee data. To build a comprehensive Employee dimension, I need to include the Point-in-Time (PIT) table that we built in the prior chapter on Business Vault.

The SQL to project the Type 1 dimension, using the PIT table for Employees is this:

```
SELECT

PIT.HUB_EMPLOYEE_KEY AS DIM1_EMPLOYEE_KEY,

PIT.PIT_LOAD_DTS    AS EFFECTIVE_DATE,

HE.EMPLOYEE_ID,

NM.FIRST_NAME,

NM.LAST_NAME,

NM.GENDER,

NM.MARITAL_STATUS,

NM.SSN,

ADDR.ADDRESS1,

ADDR.ADDRESS2,
```

```
        ADDR.CITY,

        ADDR.STATE,

        ADDR.POSTAL_CODE,

        ADDR.COUNTRY,

        CNTC.EMAIL,

        CNTC.PHONE_NUMBER,

        COMP.SALARY_BEGIN_DATE,

        COMP.SALARY,

        COMP.COMMISSION_PCT,

        SAL.MIN_SALARY,

        SAL.MAX_SALARY,

        SAL.AVG_SALARY,

        SAL.TOTAL_SALARY_TODATE
    FROM
        HUB_EMPLOYEE HE,

        EMPLOYEE_PIT PIT,

        SAT_EMPLOYEE_ADDRESS ADDR,

        SAT_EMPLOYEE_NAME NM,

        SAT_EMPLOYEE_CONTACTS CNTC,

        SAT_EMPLOYEE_COMPENSATION COMP,

        SAT_EMPLOYEE_SAL_SUM SAL
    WHERE HE.HUB_EMPLOYEE_KEY  = PIT.HUB_EMPLOYEE_KEY

    AND HE.HUB_EMPLOYEE_KEY     = ADDR.HUB_EMPLOYEE_KEY

    AND HE.HUB_EMPLOYEE_KEY     = NM.HUB_EMPLOYEE_KEY

    AND HE.HUB_EMPLOYEE_KEY     = CNTC.HUB_EMPLOYEE_KEY

    AND HE.HUB_EMPLOYEE_KEY     = COMP.HUB_EMPLOYEE_KEY

    AND HE.HUB_EMPLOYEE_KEY     = SAL.HUB_EMPLOYEE_KEY

    AND PIT.SAL_SUM_LOAD_DTS   = SAL.SAT_LOAD_DTS
```

Just like the Type 1 for Raw Vault, this one also needs a MAX(Load Date) subquery to get the most current view of the data but in this case that is done against the **PIT** table. Without the PIT table, you would need these subqueries for **every** Satellite Load Date. (Remember this is one reason we suggest building a PIT table.)

Figure 13 shows the side-by-side model of the Data Vault tables and the resulting dimension.

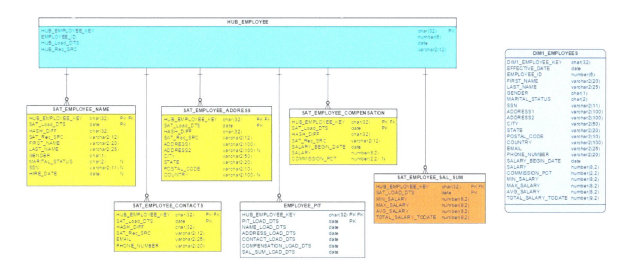

Figure 13 Projecting a Type 1 Dimension from Business Vault

This picture makes it pretty clear why we generally do not let typical users query the Data Vault directly. The Dimension is much **easier** to understand.

Type 2 Dimension for an Information Mart

Just as we did against the Raw Vault, the Type 2 Dimension on a Business Vault needs a primary key (PK), an effective date and an expiry date. The difference from the Raw Vault (in this case) is that the PK will be calculated using the Load Date from the PIT table rather than a standard Satellite table. And the Effective and Expire dates are also based on the PIT table.

```
SELECT
md5(upper(trim(nvl(HE.EMPLOYEE_ID,''')))
|| '^'
|| TO_CHAR(PIT.PIT_LOAD_DTS, 'YYYY-MM-DD')) AS DIM2_EMPLOYEE_KEY,
HE.EMPLOYEE_ID,
PIT.PIT_LOAD_DTS AS EFFECTIVE_DATE,
LEAD(PIT.PIT_LOAD_DTS)
    OVER (PARTITION BY SC.HUB_EMPLOYEE_KEY
        ORDER BY PIT.PIT_LOAD_DTS) EXPIRE_DTS,
NM.FIRST_NAME,
NM.LAST_NAME,
NM.GENDER,
NM.MARITAL_STATUS,
NM.SSN,
ADDR.ADDRESS1,
ADDR.ADDRESS2,
ADDR.CITY,
ADDR.STATE,
ADDR.POSTAL_CODE,
ADDR.COUNTRY,
CNTC.EMAIL,
CNTC.PHONE_NUMBER,
```

```
    COMP.SALARY_BEGIN_DATE,

    COMP.SALARY,

    COMP.COMMISSION_PCT,                        .

    SAL.MIN_SALARY,

    SAL.MAX_SALARY,

    SAL.AVG_SALARY,

    SAL.TOTAL_SALARY_TODATE
FROM

  HUB_EMPLOYEE HE,

  EMPLOYEE_PIT PIT,

  SAT_EMPLOYEE_ADDRESS ADDR,

  SAT_EMPLOYEE_NAME NM,

  SAT_EMPLOYEE_CONTACTS CNTC,

  SAT_EMPLOYEE_COMPENSATION COMP,

  SAT_EMPLOYEE_SAL_SUM SAL
WHERE HE.HUB_EMPLOYEE_KEY = PIT.HUB_EMPLOYEE_KEY

AND HE.HUB_EMPLOYEE_KEY  = ADDR.HUB_EMPLOYEE_KEY

AND HE.HUB_EMPLOYEE_KEY  = NM.HUB_EMPLOYEE_KEY

AND HE.HUB_EMPLOYEE_KEY  = CNTC.HUB_EMPLOYEE_KEY

AND HE.HUB_EMPLOYEE_KEY  = COMP.HUB_EMPLOYEE_KEY

AND HE.HUB_EMPLOYEE_KEY  = SAL.HUB_EMPLOYEE_KEY

AND PIT.SAL_SUM_LOAD_DTS = SAL.SAT_LOAD_DTS

AND PIT.NAME_LOAD_DTS      = NM.SAT_Load_DTS

AND PIT.ADDRESS_LOAD_DTS    = ADDR.SAT_Load_DTS

AND PIT.CONTACT_LOAD_DTS     = CNTC.SAT_Load_DTS

AND PIT.COMPENSATION_LOAD_DTS = COMP.SAT_Load_DTS
```

Without the PIT table, loading this dimension would be much more complicated as you would have to add all the Sat Load Dates to the PK calculation as well as align all the dates at points in time over history (as we discussed in the last chapter).

The resulting model for this is shown in Figure 14.

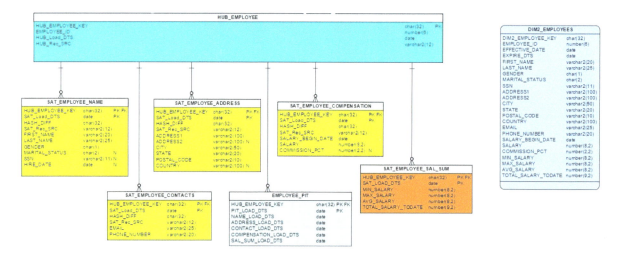

Figure 14 Projecting a Type 2 Dimension from Business Vault

Fact Tables

In the Data Vault architecture, Fact tables are usually projected or derived from **Link** tables. In Data Vault, Link tables are where we load transactions. If you think about it, a Link is the **intersection** of two or more Hubs; a Fact is the **intersection** of two or more Dimensions. While it is true that there will be times when attributes in a Hub or Hub Satellite may contribute to a Fact table, in general this is not the case.

Just like with Dimensions, there are of course Fact tables projected into a Raw Data Mart from Raw Vault tables and then there are Fact tables projected into an Information Mart based on tables in the Business Vault.

Note that if you do not yet have any BV tables but do transformation as you build out the fact tables, you are in that case building an Information Mart structure rather than a Raw Data Mart (because you are applying **business** rules to the raw data).

Fact Table for a Raw Data Mart

Building a raw Fact table, with ties to Type 1 Dimensions is very straight forward. All the **Hub Keys** in the Link can become the Type 1 Dimension Keys for the Fact (if you define your dimensions like I showed above). The **measures** (or metrics) for the Fact will usually come from **numeric** attributes in the **Link Satellite**. Since the measure comes from the Satellite, then the record source and load date also need to come from the Sat as well in order to have a complete audit trail for that data.

Because Satellites contain changes over time, just like with Dimensions, we will need to **filter** for the **most recent load date** for a given Link record.

The SQL to create a Fact from one of the HR Link tables is show below:

```
SELECT

    LMD.HUB_EMPLOYEE_KEY   AS DIM1_EMPLOYEE_MANAGER_KEY,

    LMD.HUB_DEPARTMENT_KEY AS DIM1_DEPARTMENT_KEY,

    LMD.HUB_LOCATION_KEY   AS DIM1_LOCATION_KEY,

    SMD.ANNUAL_BUDGET,

    SMD.SAT_Load_DTS AS FACT_LOAD_DTS,

    SMD.SAT_Rec_SRC  AS FACT_REC_SRC

FROM

  LNK_MANAGER_DEPARTMENTS LMD,

  SAT_MANAGER_DEPARTMENTS SMD

WHERE

  LMD.LNK_DEPARTMENTS_KEY = SMD.LNK_DEPARTMENTS_KEY

AND SMD.SAT_Load_DTS     =

  (

   SELECT

     MAX(SMD2.SAT_Load_DTS)

   FROM

     SAT_MANAGER_DEPARTMENTS SMD2

   WHERE

     LMD.LNK_DEPARTMENTS_KEY = SMD2.LNK_DEPARTMENTS_KEY

  )
```

Figure 15 displays the side-by-side model of the Link table and the Fact table.

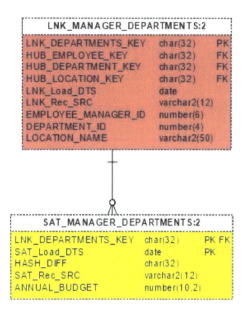

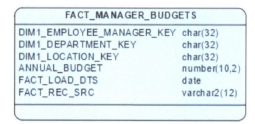

Figure 15 Projecting a Fact from a Raw Vault

Note that the measure, ANNUAL_BUDGET, comes from the Satellite associated with the Link.

With this Fact table, users can now easily report on the **current** Annual Budget by Manager, Department, and Location. With the right BI tool, or a simple pivot table, users can also easily get summary and average budget numbers by Manager and Department, by Manager and Location, total budget for a Department, or total budget for a Location, along with several other combinations.

In terms of **Agile BI**, this one Fact table can be built and delivered very quickly to get the business users looking at their raw data. And if there are questions about the quality of the data, the Fact table includes the source of the data and when it was loaded to allow a complete data quality feedback loop for checking and audit.

Because we applied no soft business rules in the transformation, technically this would be labeled as part of a Raw Data Mart, but as you might conclude, this data still provides a lot of value, very quickly, to the business users and so may be a candidate to put in the final Information Mart.

Fact Table for an Information Mart

By definition, Information Marts may have soft business rules or other transformations applied, so it follows that Fact tables built off the Business Vault would be candidates for inclusion. For the example, let's look at the Bridge table we built in the prior chapter. You may remember that a Bridge table is really a **specialized** Link that brings together the Keys from multiple Hubs and Links. Since it is a Link table, it is in fact a candidate to be transformed into a Fact table.

So using the table BRIDGE_GEOGRAPHY, the SQL to project the Fact is this:

    SELECT

```
    BG.HUB_REGION_KEY   AS DIM1_REGION_KEY,

    BG.HUB_COUNTRY_KEY  AS DIM1_COUNTRY_KEY,

    BG.HUB_LOCATION_KEY AS DIM1_LOCATION_KEY,

    1              AS GEO_COUNT,

    BG.BRDG_LOAD_DTS    AS FACT_LOAD_DTS

FROM

    BRIDGE_GEOGRAPHY BG
```

Figure 16 shows the result.

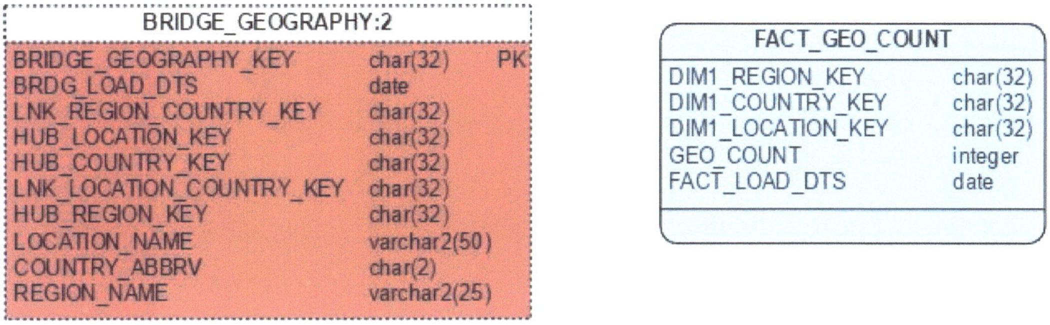

BRIDGE_GEOGRAPHY:2

BRIDGE_GEOGRAPHY_KEY	char(32)	PK
BRDG_LOAD_DTS	date	
LNK_REGION_COUNTRY_KEY	char(32)	
HUB_LOCATION_KEY	char(32)	
HUB_COUNTRY_KEY	char(32)	
LNK_LOCATION_COUNTRY_KEY	char(32)	
HUB_REGION_KEY	char(32)	
LOCATION_NAME	varchar2(50)	
COUNTRY_ABBRV	char(2)	
REGION_NAME	varchar2(25)	

FACT_GEO_COUNT

DIM1_REGION_KEY	char(32)
DIM1_COUNTRY_KEY	char(32)
DIM1_LOCATION_KEY	char(32)
GEO_COUNT	integer
FACT_LOAD_DTS	date

Figure 16 Projecting a Fact from a Business Vault

Just as in the previous example, assuming we are using Type 1 Dimensions, the Dimension Keys for the Fact table are the Hub Keys found in the Bridge table. Since this bridge table has no pre-calculated numeric columns, I have also included a "counter" column to make aggregate reporting easier. In this case, the Bridge table really is the perfect basis for building what is often called a **Fact-less Fact**.

In Data Vault, nearly every Link table can be used to quickly build Fact-less Fact tables.

With this Fact table we can quickly check the number of Locations in a Country or the number of Countries in a Region. Assuming you have the appropriate Dimensions also in your Information Mart, you of course can filter the analysis by any of the attributes in those Dimensions.

Hopefully by now, you are seeing a pattern to all these SQL statements. Whether you are building a Type 1 or 2 Dimension or a Fact table, the **basic logic is the same**: start by joining **Hub/Link + Sat** then go from there.

This is because Data Vault is **pattern-based** and the load and extract logic rely on basic SQL and **set theory**.

Fact Tables with Type 2 Dimensions

Projecting Fact tables that use Type 2 Dimensions is **hard** regardless of your architecture. You have to first build your Type 2 Dimensions, with the "surrogate" PKs, then you can populate the Fact table by looking up the Dimensions Keys based on Business Keys and the date of the Fact record and the effective date of the Dimension records.

You would need to follow the same process with Data Vault. One **advantage** with Data Vault 2.0 in this instance is that the Link tables have the Business Keys already denormalized into the structure (see Figures 5 and 6). So, when you look to find the Type 2 Dimension Key, you will **not** need to do an additional lookup from the Link table to the Hub to find the matching Business Key. This should substantially improve the performance of that load process.

Virtualizing Your Marts

A recent trend in the data warehouse world has been about creating **virtual data warehouses** and data marts. With Data Vault 1.0 and 2.0, using what I have shown you in this chapter, it is very reasonable for you to create virtual marts.

All of the SQL code you have seen and be turned into **views** in the database. All you need to do is add "**CREATE VIEW <Name> as**" to the front of the SQL in this chapter.

I have done this successfully in Oracle, SQL Server, and Snowflake already and know others who have done so as well.

So **why** should you consider using views to build your Information Marts?

1. It supports an **Agile** project approach
   - **Shorter** iterations
   - **Faster** time to market

2. It **eliminates** ETL development **bottleneck**
   - No need to write specs
   - No ETL programming or coding
   - Greatly reduces the amount and complexity of testing

By minimizing the amount of ETL coding needed upfront, you can greatly **increase** the speed at which you can deliver data to your customers.

I call that a **win-win**!

What about Performance?

Fair question.

It **depends** on many factors such as your RDBMS, your hardware, number of CPUs, and memory. But you should not **assume** it will be too slow. There have been so many advances in the last few years that we need to **test** the old assumptions! With Snowflake's cloud-based architecture where the compute has been separated from the storage, the independent compute nodes provide the elastic scalability needed to really power this approach.

So the best practice now is to start by using the views and show the data. Then if it is too slow for production, you can always tune your database, increase the size of the compute nodes (in Snowflake), convert to Materialized Views or just build out the tables the old-fashioned way.

The **key** here is you do that in another **iteration** of the project, not the first time through. In agile terms, that is often called **refactoring** – and it is **expected** over time.

Conclusion

Well, that is the end of my little book to introduce you to the Data Vault 2.0 Modeling and Methodology. In it I gave you some of the history about Data Vault and why you might consider using it for your Enterprise Data Warehouse architecture. I took you through the basics of modeling a Raw Data Vault with Hub, Links, and Satellites. Then we looked at the concept of a Business Vault and some typical constructs used there. Finally, we come to the end of the data trail with how to build a dimensional reporting layer for your end users.

I hope this has been educational and valuable for you and that you will know go forward to use Data Vault 2.0 in your work.

And for all the nitty-gritty details on DV 2.0 modeling and implementation, don't forget to order the Data Vault 2.0 book on Amazon.com. It rocks with tons of detailed examples and actual SQL Server code.

And be sure to join Dan Linstedt's new platform the DataVaultAlliance.com to find out about all things Data Vault, ask questions, and have discussions with other like-minded data warehouse architects. (And don't forget to use the discount code **AgileDW10** for 10% off products and classes on that site.)

Since things are always changing these days, you can also hop over to my website for updated listings of Data Vault books, classes, and videos plus anything new I might come up with. There might even be some special offers and discounts on this secret page. Just head over to https://kentgraziano.com/DataVaultOffers.

Carry on my friends.

Appendix: My Top 3 Reasons why you should put Foreign Keys in your Data Warehouse

This question came up at the 2014 World Wide Data Vault Consortium. Seems there are still many folks who build a data warehouse (or data mart) that do not include FKs in the database.

The usual reason is that it "slows down" load performance.

No surprise there. Been hearing that for years.

And I say one of two things:

1. So what! I need my data to be correct and to come out fast too!

or

2. Show me! How slow is it really?

Keep in mind that while getting the data **in** quickly is important, so is getting the data **out**.

Who would you rather have complain - the ETL programmer or the business user trying to run a report?

Yes, it has to be a balance, but you should not immediately dismiss including FKs in your warehouse without considering the options and benefits of those options.

So here are my three main reasons why you should include FK constraints in your *Oracle* data warehouse database:

1. The Oracle optimizer uses the constraints to make better decisions on join paths.
2. Your data modeling and BI tools can read the FKs from the data dictionary to create correct joins in the meta data of the tool (SDDM, Erwin, OBIEE, Cognos, Business Objects can all do this).
3. It is a good QA check on your ETL. (Yeah, I know... the ETL code is perfect and checks all that stuff, bla, bla, bla)

Now of course there are compromise options. The three main ones I know:

1. Drop the constraints at the start of the load then add them back in after the load completes. If any fail to build, that tells you immediately where you may have some data quality problems or your model is wrong (or something else changed).
2. Build all the constraints as DISABLE NOVALIDATE. This puts them in the database for the BI tools and data modeling tools to see and capture but, since they are not enforced, they put minimal overhead on the load process. And, so I am told by those that know, even a disabled constraint helps the optimizer make a smarter choice on the join path.
3. (really 2a) Best of both - disable the constraints, load your data, and then re-enable the constraints. You get optimization and quality checks.

So NOW what is your reason for not using FKs in your data warehouse?

I thought so...

About the Author

Kent Graziano is the owner of Data Warrior LLC in The Woodlands, Texas and is currently the Chief Technical Evangelist for Snowflake Inc. He is a certified Data Vault Master and Data Vault 2.0 Practitioner (CDVP2), Oracle ACE Director (Alumni), and Knight of the OakTable. He is an internationally recognized expert in data modeling, agile and cloud data warehousing having over 40 years of experience, with over two decades designing data warehouses and analytic solutions. This includes over 25 years using Oracle (since version 5) and Oracle tools for operational systems, data warehousing, and business intelligence. Kent is an award-winning author and presenter having written dozens of articles and done hundreds of presentations (both nationally and internationally). He was the recipient of the 1999 Chris Wooldridge Award (from IOUG) for outstanding contributions to the Oracle user community. In 2003 he was presented with The Doug Faughnan Award for his dedicated service and outstanding contributions to RMOUG. In 2007, he was the recipient of the ODTUG Volunteer Award. In 2005 he was named one of the first Oracle ACE's by Oracle Corporation.

He is a co-author of _The Data Model Resource Book_, _Oracle Designer: A Template for Developing an Enterprise Standards Document_, and _The Business of Data Vault Modeling_ (the first book on data vault). Kent was also the editor of Dan Linstedt's best-selling book _Super Charge Your Data Warehouse: Invaluable Data Modeling Rules to Implement Your Data Vault_.

Kent can be found blogging at http://kentgraziano.com, and on twitter at @KentGraziano.

Also from this Author

Available on Amazon.com:

Better Data Modeling: Tips for Enhancing Your Use of Oracle SQL Developer Data Modeler

A Check List for Doing Data Model Design Reviews

Una Lista de Verificación para Realizar Revisiones a los Diseños de Modelos de Datos

Super Charge Your Data Warehouse

www.ingramcontent.com/pod-product-compliance
Lightning Source LLC
Chambersburg PA
CBHW050935060326
40690CB00040B/550